GREAT PERFORMER'S EDITION

Arranged by
ITZHAK PERLMAN

Ragtime for Violin
(6 Scott Joplin Rags)

G. SCHIRMER, *Inc.*

DISTRIBUTED BY

HAL•LEONARD®
CORPORATION
7777 W. BLUEMOUND RD. P.O. BOX 13819 MILWAUKEE, WI 53213

Ragtime for Violin

(6 Rags by Scott Joplin)

1
The Easy Winners

Violin

Scott Joplin
Transcribed by Itzhak Perlman

[E♭ trill 2nd time only]

1st time spiccato
2nd time pizzicato

1st time

arco 2nd time

*When playing pizz. omit

2
The Ragtime Dance

Scott Joplin
Transcribed by Itzhak Perlman

Violin

pizz.

arco

(8va 2nd time for the next 4 measures.)

(loco both times)

2nd time play an octave higher

3
Bethena

Scott Joplin
Transcribed by Itzhak Perlman

Violin
4
The Strenuous Life

Scott Joplin
Transcribed by Itzhak Perlman

Violin
5
Elite Syncopations

Scott Joplin
Transcribed by Itzhak Perlman

Violin
6
The Entertainer

Scott Joplin
Transcribed by Itzhak Perlman

a tempo

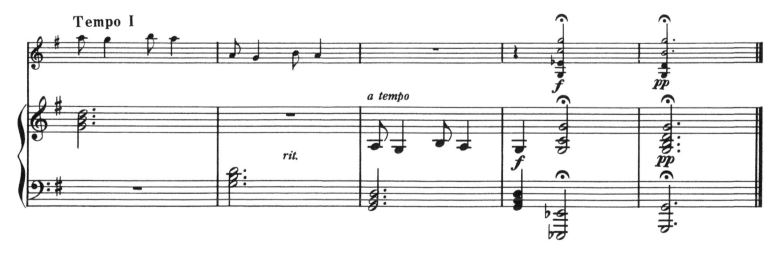

4
The Strenuous Life

Scott Joplin
Transcribed by Itzhak Perlman

2nd time 8va

Both times loco

26

2nd time 8va

Both time loco   Both time loco

2nd time 8va

5
Elite Syncopations

Scott Joplin
Transcribed by Itzhak Perlman

continue harmonics

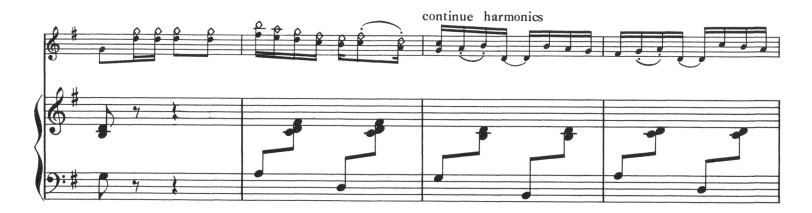

no harmonics

32

1st time arco
2nd time octave higher and pizzicato

6
The Entertainer

Scott Joplin
Transcribed by Itzhak Perlman

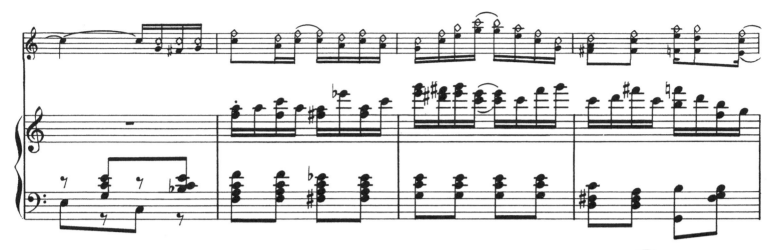

spiccato

*2nd time only
1st time Bass only